DATE DUE

Grains

Ann Thomas

CHELSEA CLUBHOUSE

An Imprint of Chelsea House Publishers

A Haights Cross Communications Company

Philadelphia

Chelsea Clubhouse
1974 Sproul Road, Suite 400
Broomall, PA 19008-0914

The Chelsea House world wide web address is www.chelseahouse.com

Library of Congress Cataloging-in-Publication Data

Thomas, Ann, 1953-
    Grains / by Ann Thomas.
    p. cm. — (Food)

    Includes index.
    Summary: A simple introduction to such foods as bread, cereal, rice, and pasta that are part of the grain group of the USDA Food Guide Pyramid.

    ISBN 0-7910-6975-3
    1. Nutrition—Juvenile literature. 2. Grain—Juvenile literature. [1. Grain. 2. Food. 3. Nutrition.] I. Title. II. Food (Philadelphia, Pa.)
    TX355 .T452 2003
    613.2—dc21

                                                                        2002000029

First published in 1998 by
MACMILLAN EDUCATION AUSTRALIA PTY LTD
627 Chapel Street, South Yarra, Australia, 3141

Copyright © Ann Thomas 1998
Copyright in photographs © individual photographers as credited

Text design by Polar Design
Cover design by Linda Forss
Illustrations © Anthony Pike

Printed in China

Acknowledgements
Special thanks to the Rice Growers Cooperative, New South Wales.

Cover: Great Southern Stock

Coo-ee Picture Library, pp. 14, 16, 18; Australian Picture Library/Corbis, p. 27; Great Southern Stock, pp. 5, 11, 19, 20, 22, 23, 25, 28; HORIZON Photo Library, pp. 15, 17, 21; Photolibrary.com, pp. 4 ©Sally-Anne Bailey, 6 ©Jenny Mills, 9 ©Christel Rosenfeld, 12 ©Bob Wickham, 24 ©Gary Lewis, 26, Stock Photos/The Stock Market, p. 29; U.S. Department of Agriculture (USDA), p. 7.

While every care has been taken to trace and acknowledge copyright, the publisher tenders their apologies for any accidental infringement where copyright has proved untraceable.

Contents

Why Do We Need Food?

We need food to keep us healthy. All living things need food and water to survive.

Rabbits eat thistle and other plants.

There are many kinds of food to eat.
People, animals, and plants need different
types of food.

What Do We Need to Eat?

Foods can be put into groups. Some groups give us **vitamins** or **minerals**. Some groups give us **proteins** or **carbohydrates**. We need these **nutrients** to keep us healthy.

We need to eat a variety of foods.

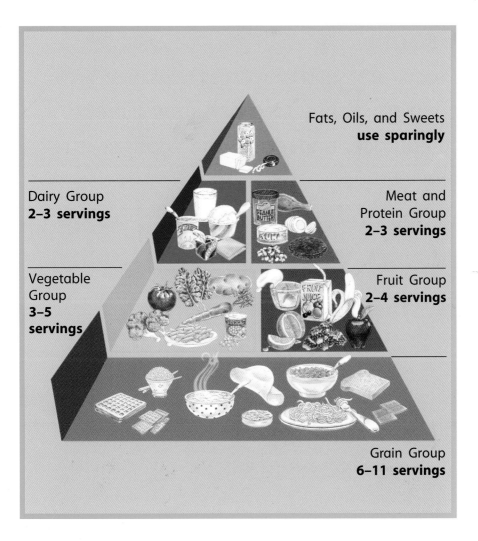

Fats, Oils, and Sweets
use sparingly

Dairy Group
2–3 servings

Meat and
Protein Group
2–3 servings

Vegetable
Group
**3–5
servings**

Fruit Group
2–4 servings

Grain Group
6–11 servings

The food guide pyramid shows us the food groups. We should eat the least from groups at the top. We should eat the most from groups at the bottom.

Grains

Grains are seeds of certain plants. We grind up grains to make foods. Bread, cereal, rice, and pasta are foods in the grain group.

There are many kinds of grains.

Rice is one kind of grain. It comes from a plant that grows in water. People sometimes eat cooked rice. Rice and other grains are also used to make cereal and pasta.

9

Grains make up the largest food group. A healthy diet includes six to 11 servings from this group each day.

Bread, pasta, and rolled oats all come from grains.

Foods made from grains are full of carbohydrates. Carbohydrates give us energy to work and play each day.

Breads

Most breads are made with flour from wheat grains. Farmers grow wheat plants in large fields.

A machine cuts wheat plants and threshes the grains.

Farmers **harvest** ripe grains. A machine separates the grains from the plants. This process is called **threshing**. Later, the grains are ground into flour.

Cereal

Many breakfast cereals are made from oats. Farmers also grow oats in large fields and harvest them with large machines. The grain goes to cereal **manufacturers**.

Rolled oats (left) and other grains are used for cereal.

Some oats are rolled flat and dried.

Rice

Farmers grow rice in fields called paddies. They plant seeds or young plants in long rows. Then they flood the paddy.

Rice paddies are flooded with water.

Rice plants do not grow as tall as most other grain plants.

Farmers drain the paddy to harvest the rice. The rice is dried before it is bagged or made into other foods.

17

Buying Grains

In the past, many people grew their own grain. They took their small crops to the local mill. The miller ground their grain into flour.

People who lived far from the mill ground their own grain.

Now farmers grow grain and sell their large crops to mills. Food manufacturers make most of our bread, cereal, rice, and pasta products. They also make the flour we buy.

Storing Grains

Grains are dry. They can be stored for long periods without rotting.

Wheat silos are usually a few stories high.

Grain is stored inside the silo.

Huge towers called silos keep grain clean, dry, and safe from pests.

Cooking Grains

People prepare many foods made from grains. They boil pasta and rice in water. Rolled oats are cooked to make oatmeal. People pour milk on breakfast cereals.

This cereal is made from puffed rice.

Flour needs to be mixed with other ingredients to make foods.

Bakers mix flour with other **ingredients** to make foods. Bread dough uses flour, yeast, salt, water, and oil. Then the dough is baked in the oven.

People all over the world eat grains. Damper is a traditional Australian **Aboriginal** bread. It is cooked on hot coals.

Damper is cooked in pans over hot coals.

In Asia, people eat rice with most meals.
Fried rice is an Asian dish made with rice,
vegetables, and sometimes meat.

Grain Products

Flour is in foods besides bread. It is in doughnuts, cakes, cookies, and other foods.

Grains are also used to make many
pastas. Spaghetti noodles are long
and thin. Macaroni noodles are small
and curved.

Breakfast cereals sometimes have many types of grains. Granola and muesli often have rolled oats and wheatgerm.

Muesli contains grains, dried fruits, and nuts.

Rice can be steamed or boiled. Rice flour is used for crackers or noodles. People sometimes throw rice at weddings for luck.

The Grain Group

These foods are in the grain group.

oatmeal cookies

muffins

bread

hot cereal

fried rice

Glossary

Aboriginal   coming from the native peoples of Australia

carbohydrate   an element found in certain foods that gives us energy when eaten; bananas, corn, potatoes, rice, and bread are high in carbohydrates.

harvest   to gather in the crop

ingredient   one food that can be combined with others to make something else; recipes use many ingredients.

manufacturer   a company that makes a product, usually in a factory

mineral   an element from earth that is found in certain foods; iron and calcium are minerals; we need small amounts of some minerals to stay healthy.

nutrient   an element in food that living things need to stay healthy; proteins, minerals, and vitamins are nutrients.

protein   an element found in certain foods that gives us energy when eaten; eggs, meat, cheese, and milk are high in protein.

threshing   to beat grain stalks until the seeds fall off the plant; the seeds are saved to make food.

vitamin   an element found in certain foods; Vitamin C is found in oranges and other foods; we need to eat foods with vitamins to stay healthy.

Index